MW01290600

The Real Life Taxi Driver

A Biography of Arthur Herman Bremer

(The Real Inspiration of Travis Bickle)

ABSOLUTE CRIME

By Tim Huddleston

Absolute Crime Books

www.absolutecrime.com

Table of Contents

About Us

Absolute Crime publishes only the best true crime literature. Our focus is on the crimes that you've probably never heard of, but you are fascinated to read more about. With each engaging and gripping story, we try to let readers relive moments in history that some people have tried to forget.

Remember, our books are not meant for the faint at heart. We don't hold back—if a crime is bloody, we let the words splatter across the page so you can experience the crime in the most horrifying way!

If you enjoy this book, please visit our homepage to see other books we offer; if you have any feedback, we'd love to hear from you!

Prologue: A Penny for Your Thoughts

May 15th, 1972

A penny for your thoughts.

Those were the words twenty-one-year-old Arthur Bremer was going to shout out when he assassinated governor of Alabama and presidential candidate George Wallace. And as he stood in the crowd outside the shopping center, applauding enthusiastically as Wallace delivered a campaign speech to the good people of Laurel, Maryland, he felt with greater and greater certainty that he would get his chance to say those words very soon. The old, familiar phrase would serve as both his battle cry and his declaration of triumph.

A penny for your thoughts.

Okay, so maybe it wasn't exactly as weighty as John Wilkes Booth's "*Sic semper tyrannis*," but then, Wallace wasn't exactly Lincoln, either. He was nothing but a racist hatemonger and Bremer would be doing the country a favor by ending his life.

Not that that was why he was doing it. He didn't care about Wallace's views one way or the other. The main thing that had put him in Bremer's sites in the first place was the simple fact that Richard Nixon was too hard to reach…not that he really gave a shit about Nixon or his policies, either. Truth be told, Arthur Bremer had never really had much of an interest in politics. That's not what this was about.

A penny for your thoughts.

For years, people would debate what the words meant, but even if he survived this day—and he didn't expect to—he would never tell. Their meaning wasn't important, anyway. What was important was that they were words he would be remembered by. From that day forward, no one would ever be able to say or even think that old idiom again without Arthur Bremer coming to mind. It would be associated with him for generations to come. It was going to make him immortal.

A penny for your thoughts.

He had set out to do the deed that morning at a rally in Wheaton, Maryland, but that had been a rough crowd. Wallace was a controversial candidate, and you never knew if the people who showed up to his appearances were going to be friend or foe. The Wheaton audience had been comprised mostly of the latter, and they heckled Wallace and his rhetoric relentlessly, and even threw tomatoes at him. There was no way the Secret Service would have allowed him anywhere near that bunch, and that's what Bremer needed to get the job done. It wasn't too much to ask for, was it? He just needed the governor to do what politicians do and come into the crowd to shake some hands and kiss some babies. That was all it would take to give him his moment, but he didn't get it in Wheaton.

Here in Laurel, though, the vibe was different. It was a much friendlier, much more supportive group and Wallace would feel safe walking among them. And when he did, he would see Bremer dressed from head to toe in patriotic red, white and blue with a great big WALLACE IN '72 button pinned right on his chest. He wouldn't be able to resist a photo op with such a big fan. Wallace would let him in close, and when he did, Arthur would stick out his hand and say, "A penny for your thoughts." And then, while Wallace mused over his answer, he would reach out to shake Arthur's hand and find that there was a gun in it. He would look back up into Arthur's smiling face with nowhere to run and nowhere to hide. It was going to be such a powerful moment, looking into the eyes of a man who knows you control whether he lives or dies. But he would only savor it for the briefest of instants. Then he would calmly squeeze the trigger and fire a single shot straight into the governor's heart. A moment later, the Secret

Service and the dozens of cops that were watching over the area would undoubtedly open fire on him, sending him out in a hail of bullets and a blaze of glory. It was going to be beautiful.

A penny for your thoughts.

Wallace wrapped up his speech and walked out from behind the 800-pound bulletproof podium. Just as Bremer had dared to hope, instead of exiting to the side of the stage, ducking into an awaiting car and speeding off to the next stop on his campaign trail, Wallace came down the front steps and approached the crowd. Bremer took a deep breath, put his hand in his pocket and wrapped his fingers around the grip of his five-shot snub-nose .38 revolver. This was it. This was really happening. He could not back out and he could not fail. Arthur Bremer's entire life had been building to this exact moment in time.

People crowded around the governor, reaching over one another in the hopes of receiving a handshake or maybe the chance to exchange a few words. They pushed towards him with such ferocity that Bremer, at a diminutive 5'6" and 145 pounds, started getting edged out, churned towards the back of the crowd, further away from his target. Panicking, he pulled the gun out of his pocket, realizing immediately that he had done so way too soon. He could barely even *see* Wallace from where he was. But there was nothing he could do about it now; the gun was out, he might as well use it. He charged forward through the crowd, gun in hand, arm outstretched. When the candidate finally came into Bremer's view, the only thing that stood between them was a little old lady. Bremer reached over the woman's shoulder, pointed his gun at Wallace's midsection, and started firing.

He squeezed the trigger over and over again, as fast as he could until the gun went click. He saw Wallace go down an instant before he was taken down himself. The crowd had swarmed around him, swallowed him up and forced him to the ground hard and fast. And as Arthur Bremer lay there, being beaten and kicked within an inch of his life, he took comfort in the fact that he had finally made something of himself. Maybe it didn't go down exactly like it was supposed to, but the result had been achieved. Wallace was dead. He had to be. He was sure he had been hit three times, maybe more. He had done it. Everyone would now know the name Arthur Bremer. And even if he died here, he would forever live on in the words…

Damn it.

He forgot to say, "A penny for your thoughts."

Chapter 1: Growing Up Bremer

The sad and lonely life of Arthur Herman Bremer began on August 21st, 1950 in Milwaukee, Wisconsin. He was the fourth of William and Sylvia Bremer's five children, which was probably at least three more than they could realistically afford. The Bremer clan was as blue-collar as it gets and twice as dysfunctional. Never having what most families would consider a home, they occupied a series of small apartments near the industrial sector on Milwaukee's South Side, each of them soaked in alcohol and steeped in emotional and physical abuse.

William worked two jobs; driving a truck for the Krohn Cartage Company by day and selling beer during the Milwaukee Braves games at County Stadium by night. He was too old-fashioned and proud to allow his wife to get a job, but Sylvia didn't seem to have any interest in working anyway. She didn't seem to have any interest in housekeeping either, as the family was regularly evicted for running their apartments into the ground. What did interest her, however, was horse racing. While William slaved away to keep food in the mouths and a roof over the heads of his wife and five children, Sylvia took his paychecks to Chicago and gambled them away at the track, holding back just enough so she could still afford to buy all the family's clothes at the Salvation Army store.

Whether they were causes or effects of their lifestyle is open to debate, but either way, there was a lot of drinking and a lot of fighting at the Bremer residence. Not one single member of the family seemed to get along with any of the others. Arthur's half-sister, Gail, and older brothers, William Jr. and Theodore, couldn't get away fast enough, striking out on their own as soon as they were able. When they were gone, they more or less disappeared off the face of the planet as far as the rest of the family knew. None of them kept in touch at all and they became little more than vague memories to Arthur and his younger brother, Roger.

Arthur and Roger couldn't have been more different from one another if they tried. While Arthur was quiet and shy, Roger was always lashing out at the world around him, often gaining the unwanted attention of Milwaukee's juvenile authorities. But unwanted attention was better than no attention at all, at least as far as Arthur was concerned. He seemed to resent Roger's outgoing nature and every so often, he'd take that resentment out on him…or he'd try to, anyway. Even though Roger was several years younger and a lot smaller than Arthur, he still usually won their fights.

Arthur didn't just fight with Roger, he also got into it with his father all the time, usually over pointless, trivial little things, and he usually lost those fights, too. The more fights he lost, the fewer he started, and he began to deal with his frustrations by running off into his own private little world. He would later write in a high school essay that he endured his childhood by pretending "that I was living with a television family and there was no yelling at home, and no one hit me."

But no matter how many times he got beat up by his little brother or put in his place by his father, his hatred for them was nothing compared to how he felt about his mother. He absolutely despised Sylvia, probably because they were so much alike. He could see in her what he would one day grow into himself and it disgusted him.

Sylvia was extremely introverted, rarely saying hi to her neighbors and never under any circumstances letting anyone inside her apartment. She guarded her filthy and cluttered home like a dirty secret, keeping the door shut and the blinds closed tight, even on the hottest days of summer. And she was controlling and manipulative, too. She criticized Arthur endlessly for never going out to play and berated him for not having any friends, even though they both knew damn well that she liked him just the way he was. Never going out meant never getting into trouble, and Roger got into enough trouble for the both of them. So she belittled him for doing exactly as she wanted, and it got to the point where Arthur couldn't stand to listen to a single word she said. If they were in the same room and she opened her mouth to say anything at all, even if it was just to comment on the weather, Arthur would get up and go into his bedroom.

The only time Arthur ever actually left the apartment was to go to school, where he proved to be a thoroughly average student. One of his first teachers described him as "a pleasure," likely because he was so quiet and reserved when compared to the other children. But a couple years later, what had been taken for an asset became a cause for concern. It wasn't just that Arthur was quiet and well behaved in class; he never did anything or said anything to anyone. Whether at lunch in the cafeteria or out on the playground during recess, he never made the slightest effort to make any friends.

In fairness though, making friends would probably never have been very easy for Arthur Bremer; he had a lot of things working against him. He was short, stocky, and wore glasses, which is a pretty tough starting point for even the most resilient of kids. But his physical shortcomings were the least of his problems. He had a strange way of walking, waddling around like a duck with his chin planted on his chest, avoiding eye contact at all costs. Whenever social interaction was unavoidable, he'd meet it with panic, laughing a weird, nervous laugh that made everyone uncomfortable. All these characteristics added up to make him an easy target for bullies—too easy, really. He was so boring that even beating him up wasn't very much fun. So most of the time, he was simply ignored.

When he was old enough to attend South Division High School, Arthur came very close to finding a place to fit in. He joined the football team and to everyone's amazement, his own most of all, found himself to be a pretty decent player. For a kid having such a hard time with life, it was everything he needed. Football would teach him to interact with people, it would teach him how to rely on others and see how it feels to have others rely on him, it would give him the confidence and sense of self-esteem that he had always lacked. With time, he and his teammates would even form friendships, or at the very least gain a sense of camaraderie. He would be a part of something bigger than himself, which is what he so desperately needed. Football would do amazing things for him…or at least, it might have if his mother hadn't sent a note with him to school, declaring that her son was "too sickly" for football and forbidding him to play.

Arthur had learned his lesson. He was doomed to his bleak, solitary existence, and settled into his place in the world, which was off in the corner, out of everyone else's way. He was neither seen nor heard for the rest of his high school career, until he graduated in January of 1969. The yearbook has his name in the index, but he is not pictured and there is no other reference to him.

He couldn't possibly be summed up better.

Chapter 2: Keeping to Himself

After graduation, Arthur got a job bussing tables at the prestigious Milwaukee Athletic Club and for nearly two years, he lived a quiet, thoroughly unremarkable life. In September of 1970, probably more out of a need to fill the hours of the day than anything else, he got a second job working as a part-time janitor at the Story Elementary School, and deciding to put the extra money he was bringing in to good use, he enrolled in classes at the Milwaukee Area Technical College.

Like in high school, he wasn't a bad student but he didn't impress anyone, either. He took courses in photography, writing and psychology, and fared no more or less than adequately in each of them, always passing, never excelling. And while many a high school misfit has had much better luck finding somewhere to fit in at college, social acceptance continued to elude Arthur. College life did nothing to bring him out of his shell. He was so forgettable, that an assistant dean who remembered him thought he was best described as "nondescript." Even when Arthur did manage to make an impression on anyone at all, it was always negative, coming across as strange and needy and driving everyone away.

Fortunately, there's always someone else nearby who's also left been left out of the pack, and for Arthur, that person was Thomas Neuman, the closest thing he ever had to a friend. Maybe since they were only together by default they weren't the tightest of companions, but at least they gave each other someone to talk to every once in a while, someone to temporarily stave off despair of complete isolation. But on May 22nd, 1971, Neuman killed himself, apparently while playing a game of Russian roulette. A local newspaper reported that he walked up to his sister with a pistol in his hand and said, "Do you want to see something?" Then he put the barrel to his head, pulled the trigger and blew his brains out.

It was probably difficult for Arthur not to take Neuman's suicide personally, whether it had been an intentional act or not—his one friend in the world had died at his own hand. Arthur felt like a pariah, as if he were destined to be alone forever. He had nothing and no one and withdrew into himself even further. He resigned himself to being an extra in the movie of life, just a blurry image filling out the background while people around him did things worth telling stories about.

But that all changed late in the summer of '71, on Arthur's twenty-first birthday. Twenty-one is considered by most everyone to be the age when adulthood officially begins, and Arthur really seemed to take the milestone to heart. He seemed to feel that it was time for him to take charge of his life, time for him to grow up. He couldn't continue to be such a little boy anymore. So Arthur Bremer set out on a mission to transform himself into a man.

One thing every man should have is his own car, so even though he was usually tight-fisted when it came to money, Arthur shelled out $795 in cash for a blue 1967 Rambler Rebel. Sure, it was a piece of junk and it broke down all the time, but that was okay. Working on the engine of his very own car is something a man does. Besides, he always felt a small sense of accomplishment every time he got it back up and running again.

Another thing a man needs is his own place. So that October, after yet another blowout argument with his parents, he decided enough was enough and moved out of their apartment and into a small, one-bedroom unit on West Michigan Street near Marquette University. The building's tenants were an eclectic mix of college students, the elderly, nurses and hippies, and not a single one of them ever had any significant interaction with Arthur. Most of the time, he ignored his neighbors and they ignored him back. Any time someone dared to say hello to him, they were met with either a creepy grin or a blank stare.

Sometimes, Arthur would take a break from his almost exclusive diet of cold cereal and venture out to the Prisma Pizzeria on Wisconsin Avenue, about a block from his apartment. There was a pretty young waitress who worked there, and like most pretty young waitresses who get by on tips, she would have been happy to flirt with him a little. But he could never bring himself to say a single word to her, not even to order his food. When she came to the table, smiled at him, complimented his shirt and asked him what she could get for him, he would just point to what he wanted on the menu, always a meatball or sausage hero, never pizza. Pizza was a food to be shared. It was something you ate with friends.

It should have been impossible, but moving out of his parents' place had actually made his situation worse. Sure, all he had ever done with his family was fight, but at least the fighting had been some form of human interaction. Without anyone at all to talk to or acknowledge his existence, Arthur began to crumble. In November, several customers at the Milwaukee Athletic Club complained to the manager that Arthur talked to himself and sometimes whistled and marched in tune with the music that played in the dining room. It was pretty disturbing behavior, so Arthur's supervisor had him pulled from busboy duty and stuck back in the kitchen where his strange antics couldn't bother any of the dues-paying club members.

Being demoted from the busboy position he had held for nearly three years was too degrading even for Arthur, and he didn't take it sitting down. After all, he was on a mission to become a man and this was a huge step backwards—he had been demoted from a job with the word "boy" in it, for Christ's sake. Furious, he complained to the Milwaukee Community Relations Commission, claiming that he was being discriminated against. Mr. Blue, the planner who reviewed Arthur's complaint, interviewed Arthur several times over the course of his investigation and though he always remained calm, Blue could see the anger Arthur was barely keeping in check with his clenched fists and pursed lips. Mr. Blue denied Arthur's complaint and in his report, he wrote that Bremer was "bordering on paranoid," and while he didn't think that Arthur posed a danger to society, he pointed out that he was in dire need of a friend…and of professional psychiatric help. He offered his own services, but Arthur declined.

Instead, he bought a gun.

Sometimes a guy needs a little outside assistance in his quest to become a man, and a gun is an obvious thing to turn to. The one Arthur chose was a Charter Arms Undercover .38-calibre five-shot revolver. It was small and compact, but had the potential for great destruction, just like him. It would be his friend and his shrink, his substitute for human contact.

At first, he was a terrible shot. On his first few trips to the Flintrop Arms Center's shooting range, he not only missed the targets completely, he also managed to shoot holes in the ceiling. Once he got the hang of it, though, it was an incredible feeling. Anyone could be powerful—or at least *feel* powerful with a gun in his hand. At last he had an outlet for his ever-mounting rage.

On November 18th, a police officer found Arthur asleep in his Rambler, which was parked outside a synagogue in Fox Point. As the cop woke him, he noticed two boxes of ammunition on the front seat next to him. He asked Arthur if he had a gun, to which Arthur pulled his .38 out of his pocket. The officer attempted to question him further, but found Bremer to be extremely nervous to the point that he was incoherent. Arthur had never been in trouble before and was panicking, having trouble communicating and even understanding anything he was being told. He came off as unbalanced, and since there's nothing more dangerous than an unbalanced person with a loaded gun, Arthur was arrested and charged with carrying a concealed weapon and parking in a no-parking zone.

The next morning, Bremer had managed to calm himself down and a court-appointed psychiatrist found him to be lucid and responsive, certainly sane enough to stand trial. Because he had no priors, the charge was reduced to disorderly conduct. He got off easy, only having to pay a $38.50 fine. But he also had to surrender his gun, and in doing so, he once again felt himself become less of a man.

Chapter 3: Joan

A few weeks before Arthur's first run-in with the law, he met 15-year-old Joan Pemrich, a student at his *alma mater,* South Division High School. Joan had started serving as a hall monitor in the recreation room of the Story School where Arthur worked as a janitor and he had taken an instant liking to her. Sure, she was young, but they had so much in common. Joan was blonde, fair-skinned, wore glasses and came from a big family with lots of kids, just like him. And she was *nice* to him. For the first time in his life, a girl didn't ignore him or laugh at him behind his back. She talked to him and seemed to actually care about what he had to say. And just like that, Arthur was back on the track towards manhood. Being demoted at work and losing his gun had been big blows, but there was no better way to feel like a man than by having a woman in your life.

It took him a whole month to work up the nerve, but on the day before Thanksgiving, he went over to Joan's house and asked her out on a date. They went to a museum downtown and walked around a beach area of Lake Michigan, looking at Christmas decorations for a while, then catching a bite to eat. At the end of the date, when Joan agreed to see him again, he began to think of her as his girlfriend.

Having a girlfriend (or at least believing he did) was a source of both pure joy and intense anxiety. He was completely unprepared and confused when it came to keeping a girl's interest. Avoiding and being excluded from social interaction for his entire life made even simple conversation difficult and understanding boundaries impossible to grasp. But Joan put up with his quirks and even found his extreme shyness to be kind of endearing. Maybe the old saying was true and there really was someone out there for everybody. And maybe for once in his life, Arthur Bremer had gotten lucky and found his someone.

Although he had saved up a fair amount of money over the years, Arthur tried his best not to spend too much of it on Joan. Instead of taking her out to fancy restaurants and showering her with lavish gifts, he would usually just give her a call, then come over and hang out at her house with her family. One time, she took him up to her room and showed him her pet gerbil, but he didn't like it—it took her attention away from him, and when they were together, he wanted her all to himself.

Joan's parents didn't have very high opinions of Arthur, but it wasn't because of the age difference. Mrs. Pemrich was twelve years younger than her husband, and all she cared about was whether Arthur made her daughter happy. And for a little while at least, he seemed to. Besides, her parents knew that it was Arthur's age that attracted Joan to him in the first place. Having a twenty-one-year-old boyfriend was a big deal to a teenage girl. It made her feel like a grown-up. Arthur could drive, he could buy beer, and he had his own place. He definitely had his uses.

One night, Arthur took Joan and her friends to a Blood, Sweat & Tears concert at the Milwaukee Arena. He had never been part of a group before, and being the oldest one there, he almost felt as if he were the leader of the pack. He was filled with an uncharacteristic sense of boldness and something close to confidence, and expressed it during the show. He clapped his hand loudly at all times and even tried out some dance moves he had seen on *American Bandstand*. He was hoping Joan would be impressed with his attempts at extraversion, but she wasn't. She was embarrassed of him.

The shine of Arthur's age had begun to wear off and Joan began to see Arthur for what he really was. The guy was a weirdo, and the more she got to know him, the more he grated on her nerves. He was challenging on so many levels; there was nothing easy about being with him. For one thing, he was constantly trying to psychoanalyze her—every time she said anything about anything, he would grill her, trying to find out what she really meant, as if there were a hidden meaning behind even the most innocuous of statements. He'd ask her question after question until she felt like she was being cross-examined on a witness stand. Then, when he finally ran out of questions to ask, he'd ask her why she never asked *him* any questions. In early January of 1972, Joan decided she couldn't take it anymore and broke up with him. Even at her young age, she could recognize that Arthur desperately needed to give and receive love from someone, and she hoped he found that person—but it wasn't going to be her.

Arthur didn't take the break-up well. They had only been together about six weeks and been out on maybe three dates, but it was the only relationship Arthur had ever been in. To Joan, it was just a teenage fling that was over before it ever even came close to turning into a romance, but to Arthur, he had just lost the love of his life. He called her constantly, begging her to take him back. It got so bad that Mrs. Pemrich had to step in, telling him that Joan didn't want to see him anymore and that he had to stop calling, get over it and get on with his life.

But he couldn't get over it. And without Joan, he had no life to get on with. But he needed something to turn to, and while maybe he couldn't have Joan, there was one thing he had recently lost that could be replaced. So he walked into the Casanova Gun Shop on West Greenfield Avenue and bought himself another Charter Arms Undercover .38, the exact same model of gun that had been confiscated by the police right before he and Joan started dating. It was comforting to have it back, but it wasn't enough. Joan had made him feel like a man in ways the gun never could. He had to win her back, and he knew how to do it.

The next day, Arthur shaved his head. It took him three razor blades to get the job done, but he was convinced that it was the best way to show Joan how much she meant to him. When he showed up for work at the Story School with his shiny bald head, the kids teased him mercilessly. Even the other janitors at the school and his coworkers in the kitchen of the Athletic Club told him he looked ridiculous. But it didn't matter. He hadn't done it for them, he had done it for Joan. But when he finally got his chance to show her his grand, romantic gesture, she laughed in his face, just like everyone else. Her parents, however, didn't find it nearly as funny and thought that Arthur Bremer had crossed the line from nerdy and quirky to dangerously strange. Joan's mother wanted him as far away from her daughter as possible, so she told him that if he came near Joan or their house again, she was going to call the police.

For the next two weeks, Arthur wallowed in his pain. He had no family or friends to turn to, no one to offer a shoulder to cry on, no one to take him out for beers to drown his sorrows. He contemplated suicide, which he hadn't done in weeks. Being with Joan had made those feelings go away, but now that he knew for certain that they were never going to be together, the dark thoughts were back. His mission to become a man had ended in failure, just like everything else he had attempted in his life. He wasn't a man at all. He was more of a child than ever. Something had to change.

On January 31st, he quit his job at the Story School and a couple weeks later, did the same thing at the Milwaukee Athletic Club, not bothering to explain his reasons to anyone. He bought himself a second gun, a 9mm Browning automatic pistol, then bought a nice clean notebook and began keeping a journal.

On March 1st, 1972, Arthur Bremer opened up that journal and wrote, "Now I start my diary of my personal plot to kill by pistol either Richard Nixon or George Wallace."

Chapter 4: George Wallace

"Somebody's going to get me one of these days," George Wallace once said to the *Detroit News.* "I can just see a little guy out there that nobody's paying any attention to. He reaches into his pocket and out comes the little gun, like that Sirhan guy that got Kennedy."

Wallace knew that he was a controversial candidate and understood the risks that came with it. He was the governor of Alabama and a vocal segregationist, although it's arguable that this stance was less about firmly held convictions and more about pandering to the white Alabama voters. He was a career politician after all, so whatever his core beliefs, he mainly told people whatever it was they wanted to hear. Although he had been less than successful in two previous bids for presidency, on January 13th, 1972, the same day Arthur Bremer bought his second .38 to replace the one that the police had taken from him, George Wallace announced that he would be seeking the Democratic party's bid to run against Richard Nixon for the office of the presidency.

Wallace first came onto the national scene in 1962, during his first term as governor, when he attempted to stop the desegregation of the University of Alabama. He stood in the doorway of the school building and physically blocked any black students from entering, earning him a solid following among white, racist men, which was a substantial demographic at that time in American history. Riding high on the attention he had received from the stunt, in 1963 he announced his intention to run against President John F. Kennedy for the Democratic Party's presidential nomination in the '64 election. It's unlikely that the endeavor would have gone very far at all if JFK had not been assassinated only days after Wallace's announcement. Wallace would have to settle for fighting it out with Lyndon Johnson, against whom he believed he stood at least a snowball's chance in hell of defeating. Before long, however, he ended up withdrawing from the race to make way for the Republican candidate, Arizona Senator Barry Goldwater.

Wallace offered to switch parties if Goldwater took him on as a running mate, but Goldwater declined. Wallace seemed to have an unrealistic opinion of himself and overestimated his value. Outside the south, there were very few people who even knew who he was, and if they did, odds were that they didn't like him.

But Wallace was nothing if not tenacious. He tried another run for president in '68, this time as an independent candidate. He kept appealing to his base by promising to put an end to federal desegregation, but he took some left-leaning stances as well, calling for increased benefits to Social Security and Medicare recipients and most significantly, vowing an immediate withdrawal from the increasingly unpopular war in Vietnam. There was some legitimate concern from Nixon's camp that Wallace would split the social conservative vote and clear the path for the Democratic Party's nominee, Hubert Humphrey, to take the race. In fact, Wallace was never really much of a threat, though the tough-talking redneck proved to be very entertaining on the campaign trail, providing a nice distraction from the real race. Never slow to come up with a great sound byte, when called a fascist by hippies, he once shot back, "I was killing fascists while you punks were in diapers." He also threatened to run over any protestor who would be stupid enough to lie down in front of his car.

In '72, he was trying to run as a Democrat again, one of a crowded field of candidates that hoped to unseat President Nixon. Perhaps realizing that the majority of Democratic voters considered him to be a white supremacist, he announced that he no longer supported segregation and declared himself to be moderate when it came to racial issues. With this tempered, if arguably inauthentic change of heart, and with strong showings in the early primaries, Wallace held out hope that 1972 would be his year.

Chapter 5: On the Campaign Trail

Prior to his decision to become an *assassinator* (he found the word "assassin" to be too boring), Bremer had never shown any signs of having any extreme political views, neither liberal nor conservative—not that anyone would have noticed if he had. But his decision to kill either Nixon or Wallace didn't stem from any burning need to make the world a better place. And why would it? What had the world ever done for him? No, it wasn't about that. He just needed attention. He needed to be recognized and considered, counted as one of the masses, and he convinced himself that the only way he could achieve that was to find someone who was already getting a lot of attention and kill that person. As he wrote in his diary, he wanted "to do SOMETHING BOLD AND DRAMATIC, FORCEFULL & DYNAMIC, A STATEMENT of my manhood for the world to see."

Bremer spent the month of March attending rallies for both Nixon and Wallace in and around Milwaukee. Afterwards, he would go home and write furiously in his diary, sometimes transcribing the minutiae of his daily activities and movements, sometimes debating with himself over which target would be the best to pursue. He compared himself to other famous assassins, wrote himself a reminder to come up with "something cute" to shout out when he killed his target (whomever that turned out to be), fantasized about killing people who had made him angry over the course of his life and imagined standing on the corner of 3rd Street and Wisconsin Avenue in downtown Milwaukee, firing his guns at random civilians. For a month straight, he poured out all his hatred and frustration onto the pages of that journal, and then on April 3rd, he put it in a suitcase and buried it in a landfill, leaving it as a treasure to be excavated. One day, it would be the biggest literary find since the discovery of the Dead Sea

Scrolls.

After burying his first journal, he started keeping a second one and kicked his efforts into a higher gear. The consequences of what he had embarked on were beginning to set in. He knew that he would very likely die when he killed Nixon…or Wallace or whoever, but there were so many things he hadn't done yet. Actually, he hadn't really done anything at all, but it was too late to do much about it now. But there was one thing he absolutely had to do. There was one thing that anyone has to do before he can even think about calling himself a man. He had to lose his virginity.

Figuring that he would be either dead or in prison very soon, he saw no point in saving his money anymore. So he took a big bite out of his savings, hopped on a plane to New York City and rented himself a room at the Waldorf-Astoria. The only other thing he needed to complete this little, yet very important side-mission was a woman. Time being of the essence, he knew better than to try to pick one up at a bar or dance club—that would take forever and he would almost certainly strike out, anyway. He had to seek out a professional, but he was too timid to approach a streetwalker, so he opted for a visit to one of New York's many "massage parlors." Maybe because he didn't understand the rules of the place, he was very disappointed when he found out he had to settle for a hand-job. When he asked the prostitute if he could "put it thru her," she said no.

Arthur was used to failure, but failing to have sex with a hooker was the final insult. He flew back to Milwaukee with his virginity firmly intact. The same could not be said for his already heavily damaged sense of dignity. There was barely a shred of it left. He had to succeed at something. He had to make an impact. If he had had even the slightest bit of doubt over whether the assassination was the right course of action for him to take, that was when it left him.

And not only had he convinced himself to go through with it, he had decided to go after the bigger target, too. It had to be Nixon. Yes, he would be harder to get to than Wallace, but it would also be so much more satisfying. Killing the President of the United States was something that would make the whole world would sit up and take notice. It had been done before and to great effect. Booth and Oswald were names kids learned in history class at school. He could be on that list of presidential assassinators. One of the most exclusive clubs in the world, and Arthur Bremer would be a member. People would know his name. Yes, it had to be Nixon.

In a few days, the president was going to be in Ottawa, speaking at Canadian Parliament, and Bremer decided that it was going to be his best chance. On April 8th, he prepared his car for the drive across the Canadian border. There was a chance that he was going to be stopped and his car searched, so he would have to hide his guns well. He lifted up the mat in the trunk of the Rambler and found a place to stick the 9mm in a space next to the wheel well. Unfortunately, in a move that was oh-so-typically of Bremer, while he was trying to wedge the gun in there, he dropped it and couldn't get it back out. Well, it could have been worse. He could have lost the .38.

The next day, he drove his car onto the ferry that crossed Lake Michigan and rode it from Milwaukee to Ludington. From there, he headed north, crossing the Canadian border and booking a room at the Lord Elgin Hotel in Ottawa.

Two days later, just before Nixon's plane was scheduled to land at the airport, Bremer pulled his Rambler into a gas station located along the 12-mile procession route to the Government House, where the president and first lady were scheduled to stay during their visit. He knew the odds of getting a shot at him during the motorcade were slim, but he had to be ready, just in case. While he waited, a Canadian Mounted Police officer noticed the American license plates on his car, and walked over to talk to Bremer. The officer was friendly, and Bremer had to be friendly back to keep him from becoming suspicious. He talked to him for a few minutes and they watched the motorcade pass by together. Although the Mountie had thwarted a possible attempt on Nixon's life, the brief conversation had turned out to be one of the easiest and most pleasant Arthur Bremer had ever had in his life. He was learning how to be normal…or at least how to appear that way.

The next day was the big day. Nixon was going to be speaking outside the Parliament building, and that was when Bremer was going to kill him. There would be so many people there, and plenty of security, but that would be okay. He would use his years of practiced invisibility to get close the president, then he would end his life in front of an international audience. It was going to be his moment in the sun, so he made sure he was dressed for it. He put on a business suit and sunglasses, put his gun in his pocket—the revolver; the 9mm was still lost in the bowels of the Rambler—and went to fulfill his destiny.

But security ended up being much heavier than he expected. It seemed as if the whole country of Canada had turned out to protest America's involvement in the Vietnam War, and the Secret Service had the area locked down tighter than any rally Bremer had ever attended. He didn't dare make his move unless he was at least reasonably sure that he could get to his target, and he never even got close in Ottawa.

It was then that he realized that he was never going to get to Nixon. It was impossible, or at least it was impossible for Arthur Bremer. Maybe if he had been a trained sniper, like Oswald, he could find a way to get to the president, but he didn't have that skill. He didn't have any skills, really. The next day, he got in his car and returned to America, a new item to add to his ever-growing list of failures. And to add insult to injury, he got a speeding ticket on the way home.

Bremer did not expect to be alive, or at least not still free after his trip to Ottawa, and he needed time to regroup. If Nixon was out, then he was just going to have to accept that fact and shift his full attention to George Wallace. It would have to wait, though, because Wallace was campaigning in Indiana, Louisiana and Texas. So from April 15th to 18th, Bremer holed up at the Sheraton Inn in New Carrollton, Maryland, licking his wounds and redirecting his focus.

In his diary, his writings became even darker and more deluded. He wrote that he was like a time bomb, and if he didn't do something soon, he would explode. He described himself as a werewolf, "changed into a wild thing." And in an apparent reference to Gavrilo Princip, who assassinated Archduke Franz Ferdinand in 1914, he wrote, "I'm as important as the start of WWI. I just need the little opening and a second of time." It's also clear from his diary that once he took Nixon out of the equation, he was never able to muster up the same enthusiasm for murdering George Wallace. But in some ways, Wallace made the whole thing even more poetic. After all, Wallace was one of the biggest losers in the history of American presidential candidates, and Bremer was one of the biggest losers in life. They needed one another. Neither one of them would ever be remembered without the assassination.

When he got back to his apartment in Milwaukee, Bremer began collecting Wallace campaign signs, handouts, and buttons. He put Wallace flyers on the windows of his apartment and bumper stickers all over the door. If he was going to go through with it, he had to be 100% committed, which meant watching Wallace like a hawk and following him wherever he went. And the best cover for that was to present himself as the ultimate Wallace supporter.

On May 8th, 1972, Bremer walked out of his apartment for the last time. He had almost gone through all his savings, so he had to try to convert the Rambler into a hotel room on wheels in an effort to stretch his last few dollars. He outfitted the car with blankets and pillows, and loaded up his cameras, police band radio, electric razor, his umbrella (which was actually meant for a woman, but did its job well enough) and a few books, including two biographies of Sirhan Sirhan that he had checked out from the library, and a 1972 edition of *The Writer's Yearbook.* Then, after once again trying and failing to retrieve the lost 9mm from the Rambler's wheel well, he hit the road, following George Wallace on the campaign trail.

On one of his first stops, he walked into the Wallace campaign headquarters in Silver Spring, Maryland, where he introduced himself to campaign coordinator, Janet Petrone. He tried to impress on her what a huge Wallace supporter he was and volunteered to help out the campaign in any way possible. Mrs. Petrone told him that they were always happy to accept help and took his name down, but when she asked for his number, he said he didn't have a phone. It was just as well—he seemed like such an odd little guy, she probably wouldn't have called him, anyway. Bremer left Silver Spring and attended rallies in Lansing, Cadillac, and Frederick. Then it was onto Kalamazoo, where he checked into the Reid Hotel and spent the night.

On May 13th, he checked out the hotel at 9:30 a.m., drove his Rambler to the location where Wallace was scheduled to speak that day, and parked in a covered lot and waited for the rally to begin. Unfortunately, Wallace wasn't going to be arriving until late that afternoon, so he had a long time to wait. It was raining outside, and Bremer had nowhere else to go and nothing else to do, and was down to his last few dollars, so he just sat in his car all day. After a few hours had passed, the parking lot attendant became suspicious and called the police.

Around 4:00 p.m., a Kalamazoo police officer arrived at the parking lot, knocked on Bremer's window and asked to see his driver's license. Bremer showed it to him and told the officer that he had arrived early to make sure he got a good seat at the rally. Usually, when a suspicious character is found in the area where a politician is scheduled to speak, the Secret Service is notified, but after a routine check on Bremer and his car came back clean, the officer decided there was no need for all that. Bremer wasn't behaving suspiciously at all. On his road to becoming an assassinator, Arthur Bremer had somehow learned how to behave like a real, live human being.

On Sunday, May 14th, Bremer traveled to Maryland. He had all the information he needed, there was nothing left to do but strike. The next day he would have two chances; first in Wheaton, and if that didn't pan out, he would get him in Laurel. That evening, he made his final diary entry, writing: "My cry upon firing will be 'A penny for your thoughts.' Copyright 1972. All rights reserved. Arthur H. Bremer."

On May 15th, 1972, Bremer drove to the Wheaton Plaza shopping mall, where Wallace was making a noon appearance, his first of the day. When Bremer arrived, he saw Janet Petrone, whom he had met at the campaign headquarters a week or so before. He was feeling good and confident, more comfortable around people now, so he approached her with a smile and a wave. "Hi, babe," he said. "How's it going?" However, just because he had become more extroverted, that didn't mean he was any less creepy. Mrs. Petrone said hello, but then brushed him off and went back to her conversation with another Wallace supporter. Feeling ignored, Bremer stood around awkwardly for a little while, then eventually shuffled away, into the group that was gathering in front of the stage.

While he waited in the crowd, which Bremer could already tell was hostile, CBS cameraman Laurens Pierce, who had been travelling with Wallace for weeks, walked around with his camera, gathering cutaway footage of the audience. He noticed Bremer in his patriotic outfit and was sure he'd seen the man before, maybe in Hagerstown on May 6th. He had been so enthusiastic at the rally that Pierce had gotten a close-up shot of him. Maybe he would be good for a sound byte, so Pierce walked up to Bremer and said, "I filmed you at a previous rally." Bremer looked back at him, pale as a ghost. He backed away, shaking his head as if to say, "you've got the wrong guy," and melted into the crowd, leaving the bewildered cameraman behind.

Arthur had been rattled by Pierce, and maybe that was why he didn't take his shot at Wallace in Wheaton. But as he made the sixteen-mile drive, something wonderful occurred to him. He had been recognized. Someone had remembered him. It was an exhilarating feeling, and by the time he arrived in Laurel, he knew that soon, the whole world would know who he was.

Chapter 6: The Aftermath

"Did I kill him? " Arthur asked. He was strapped to a gurney at Prince George's County Hospital, looking up at Police Officer Michael Landrum.

Landrum looked down at the pathetic little man, all his hopes and dreams riding on his answer. He didn't want to give him the satisfaction, but the doctors needed him calm so they could treat him for the injuries he had sustained when he had been brought down. "Yeah, yeah," Landrum said, gritting his teeth. "You killed him. He's dead."

But he wasn't.

Wallace had been hit four times, one bullet lodging into his spinal column, the others striking his abdomen and chest, but he was still alive. Besides Bremer, who had been badly beaten by the crowd, three other people were wounded. Captain E.C. Dothard, Wallace's bodyguard and an Alabama State Trooper, suffered a graze to the abdomen, a campaign volunteer named Dora Thompson was hit in the leg, and Secret Service agent Nick Zarvos took a bullet in the neck, resulting in a speech impediment he would carry with him for the rest of his life.

As news of the attempt on Wallace's life spread, President Nixon spoke with his aides about how to turn the attack to his campaign's advantage. There was no doubt that Arthur Bremer was a nut, but the first thing the president needed to know was if he was a left-wing or a right-wing nut. "Well," Chuck Colson, one of Nixon's aides said. "He's going to be a left-winger by the time we get through, I think."

That night, Bremer's landlord allowed several people into his apartment, including members of the press and very possibly E. Howard Hunt, who like G. Gordon Liddy, was one of Nixon's so-called "plumbers" and secret operatives. It's possible that things were planted or taken from Bremer's apartment, but the next day, the contents were reported in every newspaper and on every TV station. They found plenty of Wallace campaign paraphernalia, a Confederate flag being used as a rug, boxes of ammunition, a stash of pornography, and various writings and poems that were analyzed by both legitimate and armchair psychologists. Most of his writings were focused on himself as in, "A Cretique of My Life," where he listed ways to impress other people and himself. He also compared his own alienation with the civil rights struggles of African Americans in little scraps that read "My country tiz of thee land of sweet bigotry," and "My blood is black." And the media had been particularly fond of a scrawl they found that read, "Cheer up

Oswald." His car was also found, parked at the mall in Laurel, and the FBI, who had almost immediately taken over the investigation, confiscated his diary and photographic equipment. The Rambler was also dismantled, finally freeing the 9mm that had been down behind the wheel well for over a month.

That evening, when Bremer learned that he had failed once again and that George Wallace was still alive and expected to recover, he refused to answer anyone's questions. He asked for an ACLU lawyer, hoping that the $10 basic membership fee he had paid last month would make itself useful, but the Baltimore chapter found no reason to believe his constitutional rights were being violated and refused to represent him. He was arraigned shortly after midnight on May 16th, roughly eight hours after his attempt on Wallace's life. He was charged with assault on a Federal officer and a violation of Governor Wallace's civil rights, both charges carrying a maximum of ten years in prison and a ten thousand dollar fine each. After the arraignment, he was taken to the Baltimore County Jail in Towson, Maryland, where he was guarded by six Federal guards and held in lieu of $200,000 bail.

While Bremer waited for his day in court, the press dove into his past, looking to unravel the enigma that was Arthur H. Bremer. However, they had trouble finding anyone from his life who remembered him. Naturally, they went to his parents and his father expressed surprise at the whole matter—he had thought his son had been a Hubert H. Humphrey supporter. Joan Pemrich was next on the list, and after hearing about the brief but strange relationship she had had with him, pieces of Bremer began to fall into place. The more people learned, the less interested they became. Bremer wasn't some sort of ideologue with fantastic political beliefs; he was just some sad, mixed up kid.

Still, his fifteen minutes weren't up just yet, and there was an interesting ripple effect of his temporary fame. When the press was searching for Arthur's family members to interview them, his oldest brother William was exposed and arrested for fraud. William Bremer, Jr. had been travelling the country since he left home, conning housewives by selling them memberships to nonexistent weight-loss clinics. He had taken $38 dollar deposits from 2,000 women, and thanks to his little brother's actions, his scam was found out.

On May 23rd, Bremer was indicted by both federal and state grand juries. First was the state indictment in Prince Georges County, where the charges included two common law offenses—attempted murder and assault and battery, two felonies—assault with intent to murder and assault with intent to maim, and two violations of Maryland's handgun control laws. The common law charges were the most serious, as they carried no fixed penalties and could even result in the death penalty.

Afterwards, Bremer was taken before the federal panel at the U.S. Courthouse in Baltimore. The four-count indictment was handed down in a five-minute proceeding before Federal Judge C. Stanley Blair and was presented by U.S. Attorney George Beall, who assured the judge that the government would be ready to go to court in 60 to 90 days. Bremer was then taken back to jail, where he went through various states of mind, sometimes calm and subdued, other times so angry that he would spit on the guards who came near his cell.

Meanwhile, Wallace recuperated in the intensive care ward of Holy Cross Hospital in Silver Spring, Maryland, where his campaign headquarters were located. His legs were paralyzed, but his organs were not damaged, and though he would likely be confined to a wheelchair for the rest of his life, he was expected to survive. Democratic National Chairman Lawrence F. O'Brien visited him in the hospital and even though he had previously stated that he didn't consider Wallace to be a real Democrat, he would be welcome at the convention in Miami later that year.

On May 24th, with a nervous smile on his face, Bremer pleaded not guilty to the federal charges against him. His court-appointed lawyer, Benjamin Lipsitz, applied for a reduction of the $200,000 bail, but was denied. Bremer, who was dressed in a gray knit sports jacket, an open-throated black shirt and suede shoes, yawned occasionally during the proceedings and laughed to himself when the prosecutor described him as "an itinerant and transient." When it was over, Bremer shook hands with Eleanor Lipsitz, his attorney's blonde daughter and law partner, who looked a little like a grown-up Joan Pemrich, then smiled when he saw all the reporters in the audience of the courtroom.

On May 27th, Bremer finally got his money's worth for his ACLU membership fee, when the organization complained that the media coverage of his case had been sensationalized to the point of yellow journalism. They were particularly appalled that Bremer's "private writings and poems" had been printed in newspapers for the world to see. Their complaints had little effect, however. No one cared too much about the privacy of a person who had to try and kill someone to make himself feel like a man. And besides, Bremer wanted his work to be read. He relished every ounce of attention he received.

His state trial was held in Upper Marlboro, Maryland, and because of Judge Ralph Powers' upcoming vacation plans, it was condensed into a five-day event, beginning on July 31st, 1972. It was a fairly cut-and-dry affair; the defense argued that Bremer was schizophrenic and legally insane at the time of the shooting, but the jury rejected the argument after Arthur Marshall, the attorney for the prosecution, said that while Bremer was indeed disturbed and in need of psychiatric treatment, he did what he did to become famous. He had gotten what he wanted, too, but now it was time to put him away and forget about Arthur Bremer forever.

On August 4th, 1972, the jury of six men and six women deliberated for ninety-five minutes before coming back with their verdict. Arthur Herman Bremer was found guilty and sentenced to sixty-three years. After his conviction, he was asked if he had anything to say. "Well," Bremer muttered. "Mr. Marshall mentioned that he would like society to be protected from someone like me. Looking back on my life, I would have liked it if society had protected me from myself."

Chapter 7: A Fading Legacy

Bremer was sent to serve out his time at the Maryland Correctional Institution in Hagerstown. After the appeals court upheld the state conviction (although his sentence was reduced to fifty-three years), the federal charges were dropped and Bremer's descent back into obscurity began.

He had a difficult time settling into prison life. In his first six months, he got into three fights and was punished with thirty days of solitary confinement. Solitary confinement was meant to be harsh, but it was nothing to Bremer. Most of his life had been spent in solitary confinement. After those few outbursts, though, he started slipping back into his old habits of disappearing into the background.

In 1973, the diary that had been found in his car, spanning from April 4th to May 14th, 1972 was published under the title, *An Assassin's Diary*. Though a popular curio for a short while, its authenticity was almost immediately called into question. In an essay entitled "The Art and Arts of E. Howard Hunt," historian Gore Vidal noted that Bremer's writings seemed to be a little too skillful for an unemployed janitor and busboy of mediocre intellect. Vidal suggested that Hunt, both a CIA operative and a crime-fiction novelist, was the true author of the piece. The general public, however, expressed little interest.

On August 26th, 1980, the diary that he buried in the landfill was found, though it received decidedly less fanfare than Bremer had hoped for. An official at the University of Alabama-Birmingham acquired the pages and donated them to UAB's Reynolds Historical Library as Wallace memorabilia.

After Wallace recovered, he continued his political career and was elected governor of Alabama in 1974 and 1982, but never made another serious run for president. Later in his life, he began to regret some of his earlier-held policies, particularly the ones about racial segregation. He became a much softer and gentler man, and in August of 1995, he forgave Bremer and wrote him a letter reading:

Dear Arthur,

Your shooting me in 1972 caused me a lot of discomfort and pain. I am a born-again Christian. I love you. I have asked our Heavenly Father to touch your heart, and I hope that you will ask Him for forgiveness of your sin so you can go to heaven like I am going to heaven. I hope that we can get to know each other better. We have heard of each other a long time.

Please let Jesus Christ be your savior.

Bremer never replied.

George Wallace died on September 13th, 1998, not only having forgiven the man who had taken away the use of his legs, but firmly believing that his shooting had been the result of a conspiracy.

Wallace wasn't alone in his conspiracy theories, either. As with most assassination attempts, people came out of the woodwork suggesting that Bremer must have been a part of some far-reaching organization, which was fairly ironic, since if Bremer had been part of a group of any kind, he wouldn't have felt the need to try to kill anyone. Some believe that he must have had a financial backer to support all his travels following Nixon and Wallace around, but he could have easily bankrolled the enterprise himself, having saved up almost every penny he had ever earned, and having less than two dollars left to his name on the day he shot Wallace.

Earl S. Nunnery, who ran the ferry across Lake Michigan, said that he remembered Bremer when he bought his tickets, and that he was with a well-dressed man, 6'2", 225 pounds, with heavily sprayed curly hair that hung over his ears. The man had talked in a New York accent about a political campaign from Wisconsin to Michigan. He also recalled a third, longhaired person with him in the back seat of the car. However, there is no evidence to support Nunnery's claims, and in all probability, he had Bremer confused with someone else.

But there are some more legitimate hints that there was more to the shooting than met the eye. There is a 5,413-page FBI report called the WalShot Files that collects every piece of information regarding the investigation for eight years, from the day of the shooting to 1980. Also, Arthur Marshall, the attorney who prosecuted Bremer has said he still has "reservations" about the case. And some people believe that FBI Acting Director L. Patrick Gray, who destroyed Watergate records, also destroyed records about Nixon's alleged involvement in the Wallace shooting. But conspiracy or not, the impact of the event began to fade and both Wallace and Bremer were mostly forgotten.

Bremer was released from prison on November 9th, 2007, at the age of fifty-seven after serving thirty-five years. Apart from a 1980 incident where he destroyed some property and the three fights in his first six months, his prison record was clean, so under Maryland law, he qualified for early release. His probation lasts until 2025 and until then, has to be electronically monitored and must stay away from all elected officials and candidates. He must also undergo periodic mental health evaluations and receive treatment if necessary. Further, he is not allowed to leave the state of Maryland without written permission from the state agency.

While he may not have had the forceful and dynamic impact on the world that he had desired, Arthur Bremer did make a slight footprint on the landscape of society, even though nobody really remembers the name of the man who left it.

There are several significant works of art that are at least partially inspired by Bremer. The 1980 Peter Gabriel song "Family Snapshot" is often considered to recount a combination of Bremer's attempt on Wallace and the assassination of JFK. The song, told from the point of view of a would-be assassin, suggests that the action he's taking as an adult is to make up for the attention he never received as a child.

Bremer also receives a brief, albeit humiliating mention in Stephen Sondheim's 1990 musical, *Assassins*. At one point in the play, the character of John Wilkes Booth breaks the fourth wall, addresses the audience and asks "Is Artie Bremer here tonight? Where is Artie Bremer?" At that point, a plant in the audience shouts out "It was a bum rap! My penis made me do it!"

Probably the biggest impact Bremer had on the world was to provide Paul Schrader with the inspiration to create the character Travis Bickle, portrayed by Robert Deniro in Martin Scorsese's brilliant 1976 film, *Taxi Driver*. Then, in a case of life imitating art imitating life, John Hinckley, Jr., who attempted to assassinate Ronald Reagan, claimed to be inspired by Travis Bickle, who had been inspired by Arthur Bremer. All three men, including the fictional one, failed in their efforts.

Explaining why he got into politics in the first place, Richard Nixon once said, "What starts the process, really, are the laughs and slights and snubs when you are a kid. But if you are reasonably intelligent and if your anger is deep enough and strong enough, you learn that you can change those attitudes by excellence, personal gut performance while those who have everything are sitting on their fat butts."

Arthur Bremer, who apparently had more in common with Nixon than he would have liked to admit, could have learned from those words. He could have harnessed the anger and frustration of his childhood and used it to do something constructive. He could have even become the President of the United States. But instead, like so many misguided young men before him and since, he chose to go in a different direction. Convincing himself that he could only achieve the recognition he sought through violence, he put everything he had into doing something that would make a mark on history, something that would make his existence count.

Time will tell whether Arthur Bremer was successful in his efforts to be remembered. But if he is, it's unlikely that he will be remembered as a revolutionary or an assassin. He won't be remembered in the same category as his idols, John Wilkes Booth and Lee Harvey Oswald. He won't be remembered as either a hero or a villain. If Arthur Bremer is remembered at all, it will only be as a failure.

Bibliography

Bremer, Arthur. *An Assassin's Diary.* Pocket Books, 1973.

Carter, Dan T. *The Politics of Rage: George Wallace, the Origins of the New Conservatism, and the Transformation of American Politics.* Louisiana State University Press, 2000.

Wheen, Francis. *Strange Days Indeed: The 1970s: The Golden Days of Paranoia.* Public Affairs, 2010.

http://en.wikipedia.org/wiki/Arthur_Bremer

http://harpers.org/archive/1973/01/an-assassins-diary/

http://www.pbs.org/wgbh/amex/wallace/sfeature/assasin.html

http://www.questia.com/library/1G1-53409132/new-chapters-in-assassin-s-diary

http://www.youtube.com/watch?v=D3j1mwR4Xik

http://www.ctka.net/pr599-bremer.html

http://select.nytimes.com/gst/abstract.html?res=F30F17FD3F5F117B93C5A8178ED85F468785F9

http://select.nytimes.com/gst/abstract.html?res=F10614FD3F5F117B93C5A8178ED85F468785F9

http://select.nytimes.com/gst/abstract.html?res=
FB0813FD3F5F117B93C3AB178ED85F468785
F9

http://select.nytimes.com/gst/abstract.html?res=
F00613FF3E5E127A93C6AB178ED85F468785
F9

http://select.nytimes.com/gst/abstract.html?res=
F70613FF3E5E127A93C6AB178ED85F468785
F9

http://select.nytimes.com/gst/abstract.html?res=
FB071FF7355A137B93C7AB178ED85F468785
F9

http://select.nytimes.com/gst/abstract.html?res=
F50614FE345A137B93C4AB178ED85F468785
F9

http://select.nytimes.com/gst/abstract.html?res=
F60915FC3E5E127A93CAAB178ED85F468785
F9

http://select.nytimes.com/gst/abstract.html?res=
F30D15FF345A137B93C0A9178DD85F468785
F9

http://select.nytimes.com/gst/abstract.html?res=
FA0A15FA3E5E127A93C6A8178DD85F468785
F9

http://select.nytimes.com/gst/abstract.html?res=
F40811F83C5A137A93C0AB178DD85F468785
F9

http://query.nytimes.com/search/sitesearch/#/art
hur+bremer/since1851/allresults/3/allauthors/old
est/

http://news.google.com/newspapers?nid=1368&dat=19720805&id=GMwVAAAAIBAJ&sjid=bhEEAAAAIBAJ&pg=5984,1549592

http://www.spartacus.schoolnet.co.uk/JFKbremer.htm

http://jfk.hood.edu/Collection/Weisberg%20Subject%20Index%20Files/B%20Disk/Bremmer%20George%20Wallace%20Assassination%20Attempt%20Part%201/Item%2005.pdf

http://books.google.com/books?id=TWcfdyU1A2oC&pg=PA285&lpg=PA285&dq=arthur+bremer+prostitute&source=bl&ots=I5pWWv6-cv&sig=qZnB6fFKw2GCH_WdcKYPQ3bpfGU&hl=en&sa=X&ei=wfl2UfG5A8ngiAKl84DYCw&ved=0CDUQ6AEwATgK#v=onepage&q=arthur%20bremer%20prostitute&f=false

http://collections.lib.uwm.edu/cdm/picture/collecti
on/mkenh/

http://jfk.hood.edu/Collection/Weisberg%20Subje
ct%20Index%20Files/B%20Disk/Bremmer%20G
eorge%20Wallace%20Assassination%20Attemp
t%20Part%201/Item%2016.pdf

http://en.wikipedia.org/wiki/George_Wallace#De
mocratic_presidential_primaries_of_1972_and_a
ssassination_attempt

http://www.macwi.org/

http://articles.latimes.com/1989-12-23/news/mn-
414_1_assassination-attempt

http://www.washingtonpost.com/wp-
srv/politics/daily/sept98/wallace051672.htm

http://www.americanfreepress.net/html/wallace_shooter_116.html

http://voices.yahoo.com/arthur-bremer-released-after-serving-28-years-prison-652130.html

http://news.google.com/newspapers?nid=1876&dat=19720521&id=qX8sAAAAIBAJ&sjid=DM0EAAAAIBAJ&pg=7276,4172102